MEN
1950-1985

Photographs by Joan Liffring-Zug

Acknowledgments

Many people assisted in many ways to make the moments possible for the taking of these photographs.

Those who posed or assisted include Alice, Mary, Mike, Jim and Dick Passage; the Yakima Indians who invited me to the Long House; Jeanne Wiltsey; Sister Mary Lawrence; John B. Turner II; Jim, Bill, Jay, Tom, and Ruth Roach; Edmund Whiting; Peter Stamats; Ruth and Russ Nash; Fred Cochran; Robert Laker; Gerald Bennett; Joan Vifquain Liffring; William Knapp; Donna Neff; Cecil Reed; Jay Brown; Abbott Lipsky; Gordon McKay, and Maybelle Mays.

Editors who have published these photographs include Robert Dana, *North American Review;* Frank Eyerly, John Zug and Carl Gartner, *Des Moines Register;* David Archie and Charles Roberts, *The Iowan* magazine; Pete Hoyt, Don Padilla and John Reynolds, *Cedar Rapids Gazette.*

Those in the fields of literature or art who have consulted or have given encouragement include Harry Oster, Virginia Myers, Gustave von Groschwitz, Ulfert Wilke, L. G. Hoffman, and William A. McGonagle. A special thank you to one and all.

For assisting on countless occasions, I thank my sons, Artie and David Heusinkveld; my husband, John Zug; and Bill and Ruth Julin.

Edited by John Zug, Dorothy Crum, Harry Oster and Caroline Oster
Graphic designer and photography consultant: Esther Feske
Published by Penfield Press, 215 Brown Street, Iowa City, Iowa 52240-1358
Printed by Julin Printing Company, Monticello, Iowa

About the Photographer

Joan Liffring-Zug has been an Iowa photographer since 1945, the year she entered The University of Iowa to study photography, journalism, and art.

Her work has appeared in many publications, both regional and national. Her first pictures to be published nationally and internationally were those she took during the birth of her first child in 1951.

During the 1950s and early 1960s she authored four photographic children's books for Follett Publishing Company. For many years she served as contributing editor and as a photographer for *The Iowan* magazine.

During the 1970s and 1980s she has been producing many books with her husband, John Zug, principally for their publishing company, Penfield Press. These publications include *The Amanas Yesterday,* a book of photographs collected by Joan Liffring-Zug showing life in the communal Amana Colonies from 1900 to 1932. These photographs were exhibited by the Davenport Art Gallery in 1976, and toured the state for the Iowa Arts Council.

In 1981, her book *WOMEN 1957-1975* accompanied an exhibition of 28 photographs showing women of that era. Two of the photographs— *Junior League Christmas Party 1962* and *Nan Wood Graham, Riverside, California 1975*—were selected for the print collection of the Metropolitan Museum of Art.

The photograph of Mrs. Graham, sister of the late American artist Grant Wood, was taken while Joan and her husband were compiling the book *This Is Grant Wood Country.* A collection of photographs of the life of Grant Wood, compiled by Joan, was shown at the Davenport Art Gallery and is in its archives.

Photographs by Joan Liffring-Zug have appeared in many publications. She has had exhibitions in many Iowa galleries, and her photographs of *WOMEN 1957-1975* were exhibited by the New York City Camera Club and by the First Women's Bank of New York City.

Photographic Notes:
The cameras used were Rolleicord, Leicaflex, and Hasselblad. Film used was primarily Tri-X. Lighting was either natural or bounce flash.

Front Cover Photograph:
Plainfield, Iowa 1964

Note

This is a photo essay about men.

In his 1950 Nobel Prize Speech, novelist William Faulkner expressed the conviction that man would not merely endure, but prevail over the plagues of this century. Shakespeare's King Lear, stripped of kingly trappings and reduced by treacherous daughters to tatters like his faithful, wise, and frightened fool, sees man as but "a poor, bare, forked animal." My own view, on sunny days, is probably closer to Mark Twain's, that man falls somewhere between genius and jackass.

So I like this book. I like the way its photographs pay homage to the great traditions of photography, particularly those memorable human studies by Walker Evans, WeeGee, and Diane Arbus. At the same time these photos achieve this strong, documentary directness, they also combine skepticism with sincerity in a way that marks them as particularly midwestern and particularly the work of Joan Liffring-Zug.

Robert Dana

Robert Dana is the author of eight books of poetry including *Starting Out For The Difficult World* (Harper & Row, Fall, 1987), and *Against The Grain: Interviews With Maverick American Publishers* (University of Iowa Press, 1986.)

Foreword

A retrospective look at twentieth century photographs shows how far the medium has developed as an art form and as social commentary. Photojournalism came into its own at the turn of the century and is vividly documented in the work of Jacob Riis, Lewis Hine and others who, without sentimentalizing subjects, were able to capture their special humanity. Later in this century the images of photographers such as Erich Salomon, Arthur Fellig, Paul Strand, Doris Ulmann, W. Eugene Smith, Imogen Cunningham, and Margaret Bourke-White offer further affirmation of the importance of twentieth century photojournalism.

Joan Liffring-Zug, an Iowa photographer for over forty years, has played a significant role in further enhancing the field of photojournalism, through commissions for *The Iowan,* the *North American Review,* and other prominent national magazines and textbooks, in addition to photographing her world and the world of others with understanding, humor and candor.

In 1981 Joan Liffring-Zug published *WOMEN 1957-1975,* which includes twenty-eight photographs selected from thousands taken during that era. The present book *MEN 1950-1985* is again a selection of images from a vast body of work. The two volumes complement one another in that the photographs included in each establish a dialogue between the viewer and the photographer's subjects.

The Muscatine Art Center is pleased to be the first museum to present the exhibition of photographs *MEN 1950-1985* in conjunction with the images included in *WOMEN 1957-1975.*

William A. McGonagle
Director, Muscatine Art Center
Muscatine, Iowa

Dedication

Dedicated to C. Maxwell Stanley
and Elizabeth M. Stanley
Collectors and Patrons of the Arts

This collection of photographs of men was first
exhibited November 9, 1986, in the Stanley Gallery
of the Muscatine Art Center, Muscatine, Iowa, a
facility made possible through their generosity.

C. Maxwell Stanley
and Elizabeth M. Stanley
The Museum of Art
The University of Iowa 1979

Preface

These photographs of men were taken between 1950 to 1985 on assignments for magazines and newspapers, or for myself or others. At one point, I considered titling this collection "Our Heroes" because nearly all men are heroes to someone—if to no one else, at least to their mothers.

These images are not of military men or of the bizarre, the extreme, or the unfortunate, singled out for voyeuristic viewing, unless one considers all humanity poignant and humorous at the same time.

The men in these pictures were in street parades, in special dedications, at parties, or in other situations. Few of these images were posed or were taken with the care and meticulous concern of art photography or studio or product photography. But each photograph was made with passion and intensity of feeling. Many of them are "found" subjects in their own roles of action.

Timing is a doubly interesting factor in documentary photography. You slice the right fraction of a second when you take the photograph or it lacks impact and relationships and deeper emotional insights. The passing of time adds another dimension. Many photographs seem immensely more revealing of society decades after they were taken. Composition and details in the background and on the fringes of action seem far more interesting. These nuances place a person in an environment; the photograph preserves the surroundings of the past. Photographs have the potential to be icons to their era.

When I was young, there was an element of fear on my part in relationship to men—fear of physical and mental pain, anguish conditioned by a sense of childhood rejections from a variety of sources. Boys were favored both by family and teachers. My first grade teacher in northern Minnesota always referred to a boy named Robert as "Bobby Dear". No one else was so favored. My grandfather's hope came from grandsons, not from his only granddaughter. He said so.

As time passed, I came to realize that men have many of the same anxieties, uncertainties, and fears of rejection and failure that women have, and we all have more in common as human beings than we were taught originally by a society radically differentiating our roles. As I documented both men and women with my camera through the 1950s and 1960s, other women were pressing for role equality on the American scene. Photography became a way for me to explore and confront the world of men in our society. These photographs show men both alone and in their groups, not in their relationship to the women in their lives.

Initially it did not occur to me that men had a capacity for humor and for boyishness at all ages, until I was assigned to photograph a Coe College baccalaureate procession at the First Presbyterian Church in Cedar Rapids, Iowa. A professor in cap and gown stuck out his tongue. Trigger-happy with a Rolleicord camera owned by my employer, the *Cedar Rapids Gazette,* I caught this man's response to me. Would he have stuck out his tongue at a male photographer? I think not.

Initially, the managing editor of the *Gazette* thought it might be prudent not to publish this photograph. I responded that I was sending it to United Press International. The *Gazette* published the picture. The *San Francisco Chronicle* ran it under the headline "Higher Education in Iowa". Within a few days, the chairman of the chemistry department at Coe College called to say, "You have ruined a young man's career, and don't you ever set foot anywhere I am." Almost thirty years later, Coe College's art department displayed my photographs of *WOMEN 1957-1975,* so both Coe and I have survived that baccalaureate procession of 1950.

In the spring of 1951, I photographed the birth of my first child. The photographs were of a baby boy. The editors who rejected them as "unfit" subject matter were men, and the editors who later overruled them with intensity also were men. The essay was published in the *Des Moines Sunday Register, LOOK,* the *Minneapolis Tribune,* and overseas in Finland. After that, the world was never the same in terms of how I saw men in my daily life and in the images of my camera.

—Joan Liffring-Zug

Coe College Baccalaureate Procession 1950
First Presbyterian Church
Cedar Rapids, Iowa

My Son 1953
Cedar Rapids, Iowa

Yakima Indian Child 1960
Longhouse
Yakima, Washington

Gambling 1960
Yakima Indian Longhouse
Yakima, Washington

Dancer with Horn 1955
Pow Wow, Mesquakie Indian Settlement
Tama, Iowa

Indian Performer 1955
Pow Wow, Mesquakie Indian Settlement
Tama, Iowa

Tourist and Four Wooden Indians 1985
Vancouver, B.C., Canada

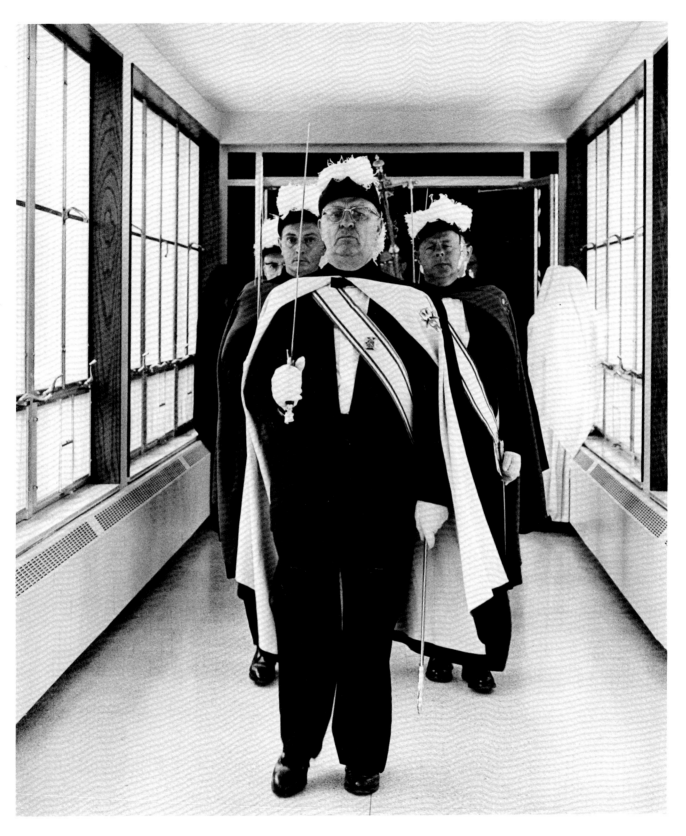

Dedication 1964
Cedar Rapids, Iowa

Street Parade 1964
Cedar Rapids, Iowa

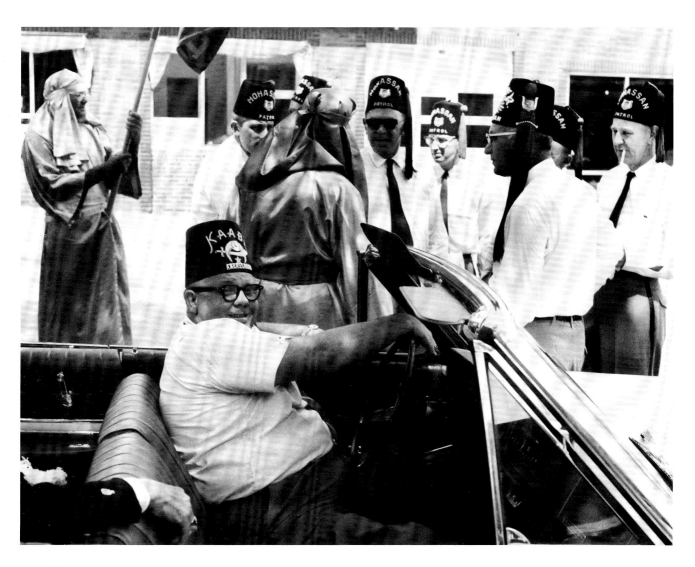

Driver
Street Parade 1964

Beaux Arts Ball 1963
Cedar Rapids, Iowa

Carnival 1963
The Great Jones County Fair
Monticello, Iowa

Young Men 1964
The Great Jones County Fair
Monticello, Iowa

Carnival Animals 1964
The Great Jones County Fair
Monticello, Iowa

Carnival Worker and Cat 1964
The Great Jones County Fair
Monticello, Iowa

Heated Winter Pool 1959
Cedar Rapids, Iowa

Man and Poodle 1961
Cedar Rapids, Iowa

Lawrence and Captain 1970
Iowa City, Iowa

Horse Trader 1952
Ely, Iowa

Penthouse Pets 1982
Des Moines, Iowa

Penthouse Bedroom 1982
Des Moines, Iowa

Andrew, Iowa 1958
Home Town of Iowa's First Governor

Auction 1964
Fayette, Iowa

Amish Man 1964
Auction
Fayette, Iowa

Congressman H. R. Gross 1963
Waterloo, Iowa

Rev. Martin Luther King 1962
Cedar Rapids, Iowa

Kiwanis Club 1961
Cedar Rapids, Iowa

Members, Cedar Rapids Art Center 1966
Museum of Modern Art
New York, N. Y.

Bust of Shakespeare 1980
Boone, Iowa

Truman Capote 1963
American Writer visiting Coe College
Cedar Rapids, Iowa

W. H. Auden 1963
British Writer visiting Coe College
Cedar Rapids, Iowa